The
Declaration of
Independence

Don Nardo

KIDHAVEN
PRESS ™

THOMSON
———✦———™
GALE

San Diego • Detroit • New York • San Francisco • Cleveland
New Haven, Conn. • Waterville, Maine • London • Munich

THOMSON
━━━━━━━★━━━━━━━ ™
GALE

Cover Photo: © Bettmann/CORBIS
© Bettmann/CORBIS, 13, 22, 26, 31
© Corel Corporation, 34
© Hulton/Archive by Getty Images, 6, 7, 9, 10, 15, 21, 25, 32, 35, 38, 39
Library of Congress, 19
© North Wind Picture Archives, 29
© Charles E. Rotkin/CORBIS, 41
© Leonard de Selva/CORBIS, 36
© Lee Snider/CORBIS, 16
© Joseph Sohm; Visions of America/CORBIS, 5

© 2003 by KidHaven Press. KidHaven Press is an imprint of The Gale Group, Inc., a division of Thomson Learning, Inc.

KidHaven™ and Thomson Learning™ are trademarks used herein under license.

For more information, contact
KidHaven Press
27500 Drake Rd.
Farmington Hills, MI 48331-3535
Or you can visit our Internet site at http://www.gale.com

LIBRARY OF CONGRESS CATALOGING-IN-PUBLICATION DATA

Nardo, Don, 1947–
    The Declaration of Independence / by Don Nardo.
      p. cm.—(History of the world series)
    Summary: Explores the roots of the Declaration of Independence, the process of writing, revising, and signing the document, and its impact not only at the time, but to the present day as American democratic values continue to spread worldwide.
      ISBN 0-7377-1034-9 (hardback : alk. paper)
    1. United States, Declaration of Independence—Juvenile literature. 2. United States—Politics and government—1775–1783—Juvenile literature. 3. United States—Politics and government—1783–1789—Juvenile literature. [I. United States. Declaration of Independence. 2. United States—Politics and government—1775–1783. 3. United States—Politics and government—1783-1789.] I. Title. II. Series.
    E221 .N248 2003
    973 .3'13—dc21
                                                              2002008898

Printed in China

Contents

Chapter One

The Long Road to Independence

I n August 1776 the citizens of Savannah, Georgia, eagerly gathered in the town square. They came to hear a local official read the Declaration of Independence, which had been written in Philadelphia only a few weeks before. An eyewitness later recalled that after the reading the crowd cheered. Then, to celebrate the birth of the United States, they fired several cannons, had a feast, and "cheerfully drank a toast." The witness added, "My friends and fellow citizens . . . let us remember that America is free and independent; that she is, and will be, with the blessing of the Almighty, great among the nations of the earth!"[1]

Similar festivities took place in towns in all of Great Britain's former American colonies. At the time, people were not celebrating the Declaration of Independence itself. They saw the document as only the means of announcing some extremely important news; namely, the colonies had separated from Britain and become a new nation.

Over the course of time, however, the Declaration became more than a mere statement of national independence. It became a symbol of the United States and its **creed** (the ideas the country stands for). These ideas—including freedom, equality, and justice for all—are spelled out in the document. Yet its many stirring, memorable phrases, such as "All men are created equal," apply not simply to Americans. Freedom-loving people everywhere identify with these concepts. So the Declaration of Independence has become world famous. Large numbers of people across the globe recognize it as perhaps the greatest existing statement of human rights and **democracy**.

Pictured here is the original signed copy of the Declaration of Independence.

Members of Congress debated and accepted the Declaration here, in Independence Hall in Philadelphia.

These ideas of liberty and justice, which the Declaration states so well, were not new to the colonists in 1776. They had long been loyal British subjects. And up until the 1760s, they had not felt deprived of freedom and justice. Indeed, Americans had been proud to be part of the British Empire in large part because it granted its citizens many freedoms and rights that most other countries did not. British subjects enjoyed an unusual degree of freedom of speech and the press, for example. Also, the American colonies had the right to tax themselves when and how they saw fit.

All agreed that this was a fair system. And as long as it existed, the Americans were content to be ruled by Britain. In time, however, the American colonists came to feel that the British were not treating them as fairly as they had in the past. Complaints and protests arose. These became increasingly frequent and intense until finally the colonists issued the Declaration of Independence and split with Britain.

Protests Against the Stamp Act

The first major colonial complaint involved taxes. Britain had recently been involved in a major conflict with France—the French and Indian War, which

Angry colonists in Boston chase the local governor after his attempt to collect the Stamp Tax.

had ended in 1763 with a British victory. The British were worried that France might start another war. So they decided to keep a large number of troops on duty in the colonies in case there was trouble.

The problem was that equipping and paying so many troops was very expensive. To raise the needed money, the British legislature, known as **Parliament**, voted to tax the American colonies. In 1765 Parliament passed the Stamp Act. This law forced the colonists to pay taxes on various paper products, including legal and business documents, newspapers, pamphlets, playing cards, and other items.

The reaction to the Stamp Act in the colonies was swift, loud, and often violent as people of all walks of life rose in protest. In Boston, an angry crowd destroyed the homes of local tax collectors. And similar protests occurred on the streets of every colony.

No Representation in Parliament

Meanwhile, the local legislatures of the various colonies met to decide what to do about the new taxes. Virginia's legislature—the House of Burgesses —put out a statement saying: "The General Assembly of this colony has the sole right and power to lay taxes on the inhabitants of this colony." Further, to allow anyone from outside the colony to tax its citizens would "destroy British as well as American freedom."[2]

Soon after these words became public, all thirteen colonies issued a joint protest. **Delegates** from

American women sign an agreement not to buy British goods until Parliament repeals its unfair taxes.

each colony met in October 1765 in what became known as the Stamp Act Congress. They demanded that Parliament lift the Stamp Act. They pointed out that the colonists had no representatives in Parliament to defend their interests. For that reason it was unfair and unjust for Britain to impose taxes on them. Throughout the colonies cries of "No taxation without representation!" arose.

Most leaders of Parliament were surprised and disturbed by the angry American reaction to the Stamp Act. They worried they would not be able to enforce it without resorting to armed force. So they **repealed**, or canceled, it in March 1766. When the news of the repeal reached the colonies, happy celebrations were held in hundreds of cities and towns.

In December 1773 several colonists, dressed as Indians, dumped British tea into Boston harbor.

The Plan to Punish Boston Backfires

The cheerful mood in the colonies did not last long, however. Britain still needed a lot of money for the upkeep of its troops. In 1767, therefore, Parliament imposed a new tax on many goods exported from Britain to the colonies. This time the outraged colonists did more than protest. They also **boycotted**, or refused to buy, British goods bearing the extra tax. British merchants lost a great deal of money. So in 1770 Parliament repealed the tax on all goods except tea.

While the boycott on British tea continued, a few colonists decided to take more drastic action. On December 16, 1773, a gang of men in Boston dressed up like Indians and marched to the local docks. There they threw more than three hundred chests of British tea into the harbor, an incident that came to be known as the "Boston Tea Party." As a punishment, Parliament passed the Coercive Acts in 1774. These laws closed the port of Boston until the colonists paid for the lost tea. Local colonists also had to allow British troops to live in their homes.

To the surprise of the British, however, their plan to make an example of Boston backfired. A number of Virginia patriots, including George Washington, Thomas Jefferson, and Patrick Henry, met. They issued a statement saying that an attack on any one colony would be seen as an attack on all thirteen colonies. Such an attack, they said,

> threatens ruin to the rights of all, unless the united wisdom of the whole be applied. And for this purpose it is recommended . . . that they communicate . . . on the expediency [need] of appointing deputies from the several colonies . . . to meet in general Congress.[3]

A Formal Complaint

Following this advice, in September 1774 fifty-six delegates from twelve of the thirteen colonies met in Philadelphia. The meeting became known as the First Continental Congress. A handful of men, including

Patrick Henry, demanded that the colonies separate from the mother country. But most of the delegates did not want to go that far. So Congress sent Parliament a formal complaint, demanding that Britain stop abusing the colonies.

A number of Americans fully expected that the British would ignore the complaint. And some of them began stockpiling weapons. Not surprisingly, this disturbed the British officials who oversaw the colonies. In April 1775 the royal governor in Boston heard that local patriots had stored some arms in nearby Concord. During the night of April 18 he sent seven hundred troops to find and collect the weapons.

Not long after dawn the next morning, the British troops met up with about eighty armed patriots in Lexington. Both sides fired at each other. And eight Americans were killed. Marching on to Concord, the British troops fought another battle with an even larger group of angry colonists. By the time the British returned to Boston, their losses were 73 dead and 174 wounded. Total American losses were 50 dead and 34 wounded.

The Point of No Return

The bloodshed at Lexington and Concord proved to be the point of no return on the road to revolution and an independent America. In the view of **radical**, or extreme, patriots, such as Patrick Henry, war was both inevitable and necessary. However,

British troops fire on colonists at Concord Bridge in one of the opening battles of the American Revolution.

even after the loss of life at Lexington and Concord, more moderate patriots did not want war. Nor did they want to form a new country separate from Britain. All they really wanted was to enjoy their full rights as Englishmen, which they felt British leaders had lately denied them.

It was not long, though, before the moderates joined the ranks of the radicals. In August 1775 the British king, George III, declared that the colonies were in open rebellion. The moderates finally saw that they would have to fight the mother country. As it turned out, one of these moderates, Thomas Jefferson, ended up penning what was then the most radical document on earth—the Declaration of Independence.

Chapter  Two

A Moving Statement of Human Rights

On May 20, 1776, American patriot John Adams penned his now famous remark about the increasing tensions between the Americans and British. "Every post [mail delivery] and every day," he said, "rolls in upon us Independence like a torrent."[4] That onrushing tide of freedom would soon crash on the shores of a bold new nation.

Indeed, by early June 1776 most American leaders, like Adams, were committed to the cause of independence. They agreed that the next logical step was for Congress to adopt a **resolution** that would unite all thirteen colonies in separating from Britain. Virginia's Richard Henry Lee proposed this important official statement on June 7. When it passed it would become the chief legal document of American independence. The Declaration of Independence was meant only to announce and explain Congress's fateful action to Britain and the world. At the time, no one realized that the Declaration would become more famous than Lee's resolution.

The members of Congress debated the resolution on June 8 and again on June 10. Then, because some delegates wanted more time to think about it, they put off voting on it for a few weeks. In the meantime, on June 11 they appointed a

Thomas Jefferson, John Adams, and others meet to decide the general content of the Declaration.

committee to **draft** a statement declaring independence. This document would be issued only if Lee's
resolution eventually passed.

The members of the committee were Jefferson,
Adams, Robert Livingston, Benjamin Franklin, and
Roger Sherman. These five men met and briefly dis-

In a rented room in this house owned by bricklayer
Jacob Graff, Thomas Jefferson penned the Declaration's
first draft.

cussed the general form the document should take. Unfortunately, none of them imagined that later generations would be eager to know their every word and gesture. So they kept no notes and the contents of their conversation will never be known. What is certain is that Franklin, Adams, Livingston, and Sherman asked Jefferson to prepare the all-important first **draft**.

Jefferson never described the actual writing of the draft in any detail, and the exact circumstances surrounding this process remain uncertain. However, modern historians have pieced together certain basic facts. First, he completed the initial work sometime between June 12 and June 28, 1776. Also, he worked in a parlor on the second floor of a rented house on the corner of Philadelphia's Seventh and Market Streets. Jefferson himself designed the parlor's now famous folding desk. It is also fairly certain that he used a goose quill pen that had to be redipped in an inkwell after every one or two words.

The Document's Major Premise

The Declaration's form and content reveal Jefferson's overall purpose and strategy. His format was a kind of argument called a **syllogism**, which attempts to persuade someone by using simple, logical reasoning. The form consists of three parts. The first is the major premise, or idea, which is stated in the introduction; second comes the minor premise, which is stated and developed in the main body of the work;

and finally comes the conclusion, which follows logically from the first two parts. In such an argument, if premise A and premise B are true, then the conclusion, C, must be the logical and natural result.

Jefferson's purpose was to convince the world that the colonies' separation from Britain was right and justified. He also wanted to summarize the democratic political ideas of the new nation about to be born. For his major premise, therefore, he chose a daringly democratic concept. Namely, just governments are established on equal rights and the consent of those governed. "We hold these truths to be sacred and undeniable," the second paragraph of the draft began, "that all men are created equal and independent, that from that equal creation they derive rights inherent and **inalienable** [not to be surrendered]."[5] To make sure these rights are secure, he continued, "governments are instituted among men." These governments derive "their just powers from the consent of the governed"; and if a government denies its citizens these rights, it is the right of those citizens to alter or abolish that government and institute a new, fairer one.

The strength of the first premise was that it was "sacred and undeniable." (Jefferson later changed this phrase to "self-evident.") In other words, it constituted a fundamental human moral truth that needed little or no demonstration. And that made it instantly understandable to all people of reason and good will.

The Sources of Jefferson's Ideas

Jefferson did not invent these democratic ideas. Rather, he had absorbed them during many years of reading and discussion. Like many other educated people at the time, he was deeply impressed by the European Enlightenment. This was a movement of thinkers and writers. Most were English and French and lived in the seventeenth and eighteenth centuries. They strongly supported religious freedom, the use of reason and science, fair government, and basic human rights, including freedom of speech and expression.

Of these thinkers, Jefferson was most influenced by Englishman John Locke (1632–1704). Locke

The ideas of English philosopher John Locke (pictured) strongly influenced Thomas Jefferson.

wrote that nations ruled by kings usually denied citizens many natural human rights. It would be better, he said, if all governments were based on the consent of those governed.

Jefferson achieved two great things. First, he collected important ideas from Locke and many other diverse sources and brought them together in one document. Second, because Jefferson was a gifted writer he was able to express these concepts in terms that anyone anywhere could easily understand.

The Minor Premise and Conclusion

When he had finished stating the major premise, Jefferson tackled the minor one: that the British king and Parliament had repeatedly denied the "undeniable" rights of the American colonists. Developing this premise filled up most of the main body of the Declaration. It consisted of a list of eighteen charges against the king. Among them was: "He has kept among us in times of peace standing armies and ships of war without the consent of our legislatures."

The conclusion of Jefferson's argument followed from the two ideas he had "proved." Thus, A: Just governments do not deny their citizens basic rights such as equality; and if they do, citizens have the right to abolish those governments. B: The British king has repeatedly denied his American subjects their rights as Englishmen. Therefore, C: The colonists are justified in parting with Britain and declaring "these colonies to be free and independent states."

In the Declaration, Thomas Jefferson listed grievances against the British king, George III, pictured here.

A Few Initial Revisions

Having finished the Declaration's original draft, on June 25 or 26 Jefferson showed it to two other members of the committee. He later recalled that

Thomas Jefferson (right) shows the Declaration's rough draft to Benjamin Franklin.

before I reported it [the draft] to the committee, I communicated it *separately* to Dr. Franklin and Mr. Adams, requesting their corrections, because they were the two members of whose judgments and **amendments** [changes] I wished most to have the benefit before presenting it to the [entire] committee.[6]

The three men met, likely at least twice and possibly three or four times. They made a total of twenty-six changes, all of them minor. Livingston and Sherman then probably examined the document and approved it.

By this time, one thing must have been clear to Jefferson's four colleagues. The document he had created largely on his own and in little more than ten days went far beyond what anyone had expected. It was more than a simple list of reasons for the colonies to separate from the mother country. Indeed, the Declaration was a moving statement of human equality, rights, and values.

The question was whether anyone but the members of Congress would ever see this profound statement. Congress still had to approve it. And that could not happen until Lee's resolution on independence had passed. If the colonies could not all agree to the split with Britain, the Declaration would remain a rough draft, perhaps to be tossed into a drawer and forgotten. All involved agreed that Congress needed to act without further delay.

Chapter ⬤ Three

Debating and Signing the Declaration

Fortunately for future generations, the Declaration of Independence did not end up forgotten in some drawer or cellar. By June 28, 1776, Jefferson and the other members of his committee had made their initial revisions in the document's rough draft. And on that day they submitted it to Congress.

However, as expected, the delegates temporarily put the matter aside, as debating Lee's resolution was more pressing. That work began on July 1. The next day the delegates voted on and passed the resolution. Thus, contrary to popular belief, July 2, 1776, and not July 4, was the actual day the United States was born. In time, July 4 would become more memorable, mainly because of the many moving and powerful words and ideas in the Declaration.

Some Minor Changes

After the patriots passed Lee's resolution on July 2, the Declaration was their next order of business. Debate on the wording of Jefferson's rough draft began that day. And the revision process continued for almost three solid days, during which Congress made a number of changes.

Some of these changes were relatively minor. For instance, Jefferson had written in his rough draft, "and such is now the necessity which constrains

The members of the committee meet one last time just prior to showing the Declaration to Congress.

them [the colonies] to expunge their former systems of governments." Congress substituted the word "alter" for "expunge."[7]

Other minor changes consisted of cutting out certain words and phrases to simplify the text; or adding new words and phrases to make an idea clearer or more forceful. For example, Jefferson had

Thomas Jefferson (standing), Ben Franklin, and John Adams confer while Congress debates the wording of the Declaration.

accused the king of "transporting large armies . . . to complete the works of death, **desolation** [ruin] and tyranny already begun with circumstances of cruelty and **perfidy** [treachery] unworthy the head of a civilized nation." The delegates felt this phrase was not strong enough. In their view, it did not adequately convey their sense of outrage at such warlike acts. So they put in nine new words, making the phrase more powerful. It now read: "to complete the works of death, desolation and tyranny already begun with circumstances of cruelty and perfidy scarcely paralleled in the most barbarous ages, and totally unworthy the head of a civilized nation."[8]

Larger Revisions

A few of the changes Congress made in Jefferson's rough draft were larger, consisting of cutting out entire paragraphs. Mostly, these paragraphs contained strong criticisms of Britain. Some were aimed directly at Parliament and British leaders. For example, Jefferson complained about certain British leaders who wanted to keep America under Parliament's thumb. He called them "the disturbers of our harmony." These men, he said, had enacted numerous laws (including the Coercive Acts) that had placed unfair burdens on the colonies. Even worse, they had recently sent soldiers "to invade and destroy us." Considering these facts, Jefferson reasoned, it was necessary for Americans to condemn the British and "to forget our former love for them."[9]

Jefferson then added a touch of regret, reminding the British of what they had lost: "We might have been a free and great people together." But because sharing the concept of freedom was "below their [i.e., British] dignity," the Americans would gladly tread "the road to happiness"[10] on their own.

Many members of Congress felt uneasy about these forceful statements. In particular, they were worried they might offend the few British citizens and leaders who agreed that Britain had abused the colonies. According to this view, it would be safer and wiser to omit such passages. And the Declaration should focus on denouncing the king, who was in a sense more of a symbol than a person.

The Anti-Slavery Clause

By far the most controversial change Congress made in Jefferson's rough draft concerned his attack on slavery. In his view, slavery was morally wrong. And in establishing their new nation, he said, American leaders should take some kind of moral stand. To this end, he included the following clause in his rough draft:

> He [the king] has waged cruel war against human nature itself, violating its most sacred rights of life and liberty in the persons of a distant people who never offended him [i.e., black Africans], captivating and carrying them into slavery in another hemisphere. . . . De-

Thomas Jefferson hoped the new nation would outlaw slavery but Congress deleted his anti-slavery clause from the Declaration.

termined to keep open a market where men should be bought and sold, he has . . . [suppressed] every legislative attempt to prohibit or to restrain this [awful] commerce . . . [and] he is now exciting those very people [the slaves] to rise in arms against us.[11]

This remarkable assault on the slave trade took many of the patriots by surprise. Those from southern states, especially South Carolina and Georgia, which had many slaves, were particularly upset. They strongly opposed stopping or even slowing the trade. And they would not allow such liberal words and ideas to appear in an important American public document. Jefferson later recalled that some delegates from the North also favored deleting these words; the sad fact was that many ships from northern states were involved in the profitable trade in human cargo. So, to Jefferson's regret, Congress cut out the anti-slavery clause.

The Signing Process

Congress finished its revision of the Declaration of Independence late in the day on July 4, 1776. The delegates did not all sign it that day, as so often pictured in later paintings, books, and movies. The actual signing process was much more complex and drawn out. First, on July 4, twelve of the thirteen states agreed to adopt the Declaration as a written expression of Lee's resolution on independence. The delegates from New York did not vote. And that state's legislature did not approve the document until July 15.

Meanwhile, sometime between July 5 and 7 several copies of the Declaration were printed and sent to the various state legislatures. On July 8 the Declaration's first public reading took place in the yard of Philadelphia's state house. The large crowd that had gathered there cheered loudly. Then there was a parade and bells rang through most of the night. Similar scenes occurred all across America in the weeks that followed.

These few initial printed copies of the Declaration bore no signatures. Apparently, the only people who signed the document on July 4 were John

Patriot John Dixon reads the Declaration in the yard of Philadelphia's state house on July 8, 1776.

John Hancock, president of Congress, signs the Declaration on July 4, 1776.

Hancock as the president of Congress and possibly Charles Thomson, the congressional secretary. It was not until July 19 that Congress ordered the Declaration to be signed by all the members. The formal signing ceremony took place on August 2. Jefferson, the principal author, probably signed it that day. However, some of his congressional colleagues were unable to attend the ceremony. So they signed the document in the following few days and weeks. In all, fifty-six members of Congress signed it, although their signatures were not made public until January 1777. This turned out to be only the beginning of the Declaration's history, one that no one at the time foresaw.

Chapter Four

The Declaration's Living Legacy

Fortunately, the original copy of the Declaration of Independence that Jefferson and his fellow patriots signed has survived intact. Public officials frequently moved it from one American city to another until 1952. In that year it went on display in the exhibition hall of the National Archives in Washington, D.C., where it remains. Tens of thousands of people go there each year to see this renowned and revered relic.

During the 176 years that elapsed before the Declaration found its permanent home, the influence of its democratic principles spread far and wide. The men who signed the document created the world's first modern democracy. That nation then went on to defeat Britain, at the time the

This famous painting depicts the signing of the Declaration of Independence in 1776.

strongest nation on earth. These events set an inspiring example for others around the world who dreamed of freedom and independence.

The question was whether this brave new democracy could survive in a world still dominated by powerful kings. At first, many foreign leaders thought it could not. However, the United States proved these doubters wrong by surviving numerous wars and other crises. Over the years it showed the world that a government ruled by the people could work and prosper. And many millions of people around the world were able to exercise the right to happiness that Jefferson called a primary human birthright in the Declaration.

The French Revolution

As it turned out, France was the first foreign nation to benefit from the Declaration's liberal principles. At the time of the American Revolution, France was approaching the brink of economic and social disaster. For years the French people had been growing more and more unhappy. This was partly because the country's kings and nobles enjoyed great wealth while most of the common people lived in extreme poverty. The people could not choose their leaders and came to see the government as unjust and oppressive.

It is not surprising, therefore, that many French were fascinated by the American Revolution. They saw that the war had been fought to achieve the

After hearing the words of the Declaration, patriots in New York topple a statue of King George III.

stirring democratic principles stated in the Declaration of Independence. Jefferson himself later recalled: "The American Revolution seems . . . to have awakened the thinking part of the French nation . . . from the sleep of **despotism** [tyranny] in which they were sunk."[12]

The Declaration of Independence and American Revolution set an example for French revolutionaries. These factors did not cause or incite the French Revolution, which erupted in 1789. But they did show the French that such a fight could actually be waged and won by people with a just cause. "America has given us an example," wrote the Marquis de Condorcet, a noted French thinker. "The act which

A mob of French citizens storms Paris's Bastille prison, symbol of the abuses of the French nobility.

declares its independence [i.e., the Declaration of Independence] is a simple and sublime exposition [statement] of those rights so sacred and so long forgotten."[13]

An Amazing Success Story

The French Revolution overthrew France's monarchy. Unfortunately, however, the country remained in turmoil and took several decades to achieve real democracy. Meanwhile, the democratic principles of the American and French struggles inspired revolutions in many other lands.

In 1810 local patriots in Venezuela, in South America, began a revolution to gain independence from their mother country, Spain. Democratic governments were also established in Argentina, also in South America, in 1816, and Liberia, in western Africa, in 1847. In 1848, in Europe, the Austrian people rose up and forced their emperor off his throne; his successor had to adopt fairer, more liberal political policies. In Hungary, the people demanded and won a new constitution that recognized several basic human rights. And demands for political reform echoed through Germany, Italy, and many other nations.

This trend toward democracy continued and gained speed in the twentieth century. Dozens of democracies were established around the world in that century. The total reached seventy-five in 1992. And in the majority of cases, the United

Soldiers of the infant U.S. Army cheer after hearing
a reading of the Declaration.

States sponsored, aided, and inspired the founding
of these nations.

These events happened partly because the United
States became a military superpower in these years
and it used its great authority and prestige to encour-
age the spread of democracy. Even more important
was the tremendous success of the nation's market
economy and high living standards. This success was
achieved largely through the spirit of free private en-

terprise. And free enterprise is one of the fruits of a long-lived and open democratic system.

Many other nations wanted to imitate or share in this amazing success story. As a result, the United States was able to export to these countries many of the democratic ideas mentioned in the Declaration of Independence. One way was to make sure that such ideas were included in important international agreements. The most famous example is the charter of the United Nations. It contains the Declaration

The Liberty Bell rings in Philadelphia to celebrate American independence from Britain.

of Human Rights, adopted on December 6, 1948, which proclaims in part:

> All human beings are born free and equal in dignity and rights. They are endowed with reason and conscience and should act towards one another in a spirit of brotherhood. . . . Everyone has the right to life, liberty, and security of person . . . [and] freedom of opinion and expression.[14]

The Revolution Continues

Thus, American democratic values eventually spread around the globe. Yet nowhere have these values had stronger influence than in the United States itself. What Jefferson and his fellows did not realize at the time was that their revolution did not end in 1783 with their defeat of Britain. That event marked merely the end of the fight for political independence.

In reality, a larger revolution had just begun. The founding fathers had created a new and daring kind of government based on the ideas of equality and opportunity for all. At first these concepts existed mainly on paper. Slavery still existed, for example. And women were not allowed to vote. But over time increasing numbers of Americans came to see freedom and equality as their birthright. In each new generation, group after group demanded their civil rights. And finally, after a long and diffi-

Fireworks light up the Statue of Liberty in New York Harbor during a modern July 4th celebration.

cult struggle, they began to enjoy these rights. Slavery was abolished, women gained the right to vote, and laws were passed against racial, ethnic, religious, and age **discrimination**.

Thus, in breaking away from Britain, the American patriots did more than create a new nation. They also set in motion a mighty democratic revolution that still shows no signs of letting up. This struggle to transform the ideals of the Declaration of Independence into reality will not cease until everyone everywhere has achieved true equality. That is the powerful living legacy of the document.

Notes

Chapter One: The Long Road to Independence

1. Quoted in Peter Force, ed., *American Archives,* vol. 1. Washington, DC: Clarke and Force, 1837–1846, p. 882.

2. Quoted in Max Beloff, ed., *The Debate on the American Revolution, 1761–1783.* London: Adam and Charles Black, 1960, p. 71.

3. Quoted in Julian P. Boyd, ed., *The Papers of Thomas Jefferson,* vol. 1. Princeton: Princeton University Press, 1950–1954, p. 108.

Chapter Two: A Moving Statement of Human Rights

4. Quoted in Henry S. Commager and Richard B. Morris, eds., *The Spirit of 'Seventy-Six: The Story of the American Revolution as Told by Participants,* vol. 1. New York: Bobbs-Merrill, 1958, p. 295.

5. This and the following several quotes from Jefferson's rough draft are taken from Carl Becker, *The Declaration of Independence: A Study in the History of Political Ideas.* New York: Harcourt, Brace & Co., 1922, pp. 141–51.

6. Quoted in Paul L. Ford, *The Writings of Thomas Jefferson,* vol. 10. New York: Putnam, 1892–1899, p. 266.

Chapter Three: Debating and Signing the Declaration

7. See Adrienne Koch and William Peden, eds., *The Life and Selected Writings of Thomas Jefferson.* New York: Random House, 1944, pp. 22–23.

8. See Koch and Peden, *Life and Selected Writings of Thomas Jefferson,* p. 25.

9. See Koch and Peden, *Life and Selected Writings of Thomas Jefferson,* pp. 26–27.

10. See Koch and Peden, *Life and Selected Writings of Thomas Jefferson,* pp. 26–27.

11. Quoted in Becker, *Declaration of Independence,* pp. 212–13.

Chapter Four: The Declaration's Living Legacy

12. Quoted in Koch and Peden, *Life and Selected Writings of Thomas Jefferson,* p. 72.

13. Quoted in Becker, *Declaration of Independence,* pp. 230–31.

14. Quoted in Diane Ravitch, ed., *The American Reader: Words That Moved a Nation.* New York: HarperCollins, 1990, pp. 202–204.

Glossary

amendment: A change or addition, usually to a written document.

boycott: To refuse to buy certain goods in an effort to punish the seller.

creed: A set of basic beliefs.

delegate: A person representing a town, state, or other group at a joint meeting.

democracy: A form of government in which power is held by the people or their representatives.

desolation: Ruin.

despotism: Tyranny.

discrimination: Treating someone differently, usually badly, for reasons such as race, ethnic background, religion, or gender.

draft: An early version of a written work; or to write such a document.

inalienable: Incapable of being surrendered or given away.

Parliament: Britain's legislature, similar in some ways to the U.S. Congress.

perfidy: Treachery or double dealing.

radical: Drastic or revolutionary.

repeal: To cancel or eliminate.

resolution: A proposal, usually in a meeting or legislature.

syllogism: A kind of argument that attempts to persuade someone by using simple, logical reasoning. It usually consists of three parts—a major premise, minor premise, and conclusion.

For Further Exploration

Herbert M. Atherton and J. Jackson Barlow, eds., *1791–1991, The Bill of Rights and Beyond*. Washington, DC: Commission on the Bicentennial of the United States Constitution, 1990. This very handsomely mounted book, which is available in most schools and libraries, features many stunning photos and drawings that perfectly highlight the readable text summarizing the impact of the original ten amendments to the Constitution.

Kathy Furgang, *The Declaration of Independence and John Adams of Massachusetts*. New York: Powerkids Press, 2002. Covers Adams's role in the events of 1776, including his work on the drafting committee of the Declaration.

——, *The Declaration of Independence and Richard Henry Lee of Virginia*. New York: Powerkids Press, 2002. Another of Ms. Furgang's volumes about the creation of the United States, this one focuses on Lee, whose resolution made the colonies' split with Britain official.

Bonnie L. Lukes, *The American Revolution*. San Diego: Lucent Books, 1996. A well-written history of the American war for independence, highlighted by numerous quotes from primary and secondary historical and literary sources describing the conflict and the period. Suitable for junior high, high school, and adult non-specialist readers.

Don Nardo, *The American Revolution*. San Diego: KidHaven Press, 2002. A concise, colorfully illustrated overview of the American war for independence written for basic readers.

————, *Democracy*. San Diego: Lucent Books, 1994. Traces the origins and development of democratic thought and practice from ancient Athens and the Roman Republic through the Magna Carta; the development of the English Parliament; the English Bill of Rights; the ideas of Locke, Rousseau, Montesquieu, Mills, and other advocates of human rights; the American Revolution and establishment of the U.S. Constitution; the French Revolution, and the spread of democracy in the modern world.

————, *Thomas Jefferson*. New York: Franklin Watts, 2003. This biography of Jefferson, aimed at junior high school readers, includes his role as principal author of the Declaration of Independence as well as his other contributions to the formation of the early United States.

Walter Olesky, *The Boston Tea Party*. New York: Franklin Watts, 1993. The events and personalities shaping the famous incident that provoked Parliament into punishing Boston and thereby fatally escalated tensions between the colonies and Britain are recounted here in a simple format for basic readers.

Index